Kids Chat
God's Spirit

If you lose a balloon into the sky, just imagine it is a gift going up to God!

Family devotional inspired by God's word
by Kristin Gembala & Patti Seacrist

KIDS CHAT GOD'S SPIRIT: FAMILY DEVOTIONAL INSPIRED BY GOD'S WORD
PUBLISHED BY APPRECIATE THE WORLD, INC.

ISBN 13: 978-0-9791195-0-7
ISBN 10: 0-9791195-0-2

Written by Kristin Gembala and Patti Seacrist, inspired by our children and their powerful voices that teach us every day. Illustrated by our children. Relentless thanks to our husbands who support, give and listen everyday!

Contact us by e-mail at: kidschat@appreciatetheworld.com
www.appreciatetheworld.com

All verses from The NIV Adventure Bible Zonderkidz

Cover illustration by Alyssa Gembala

Deuteronomy 6:6-7

These commandments that I give you today are to be upon your hearts. Impress them on your children. Talk about them when you sit at home and when you walk along the road, **when you lie down** and when you get up.

    This is a "night-stand" book. It is designed to sit on a child's night-stand so it can be easily picked up at night, when children give their parents crucial information about their day. The book is designed to read one page per night with each page taking 2 – 5 minutes. This gives busy families a chance to talk about what is important in their lives.

    Our families are precious. If any one child or family can spend a small amount of time reading and conversing about some important values in life, then this book has done what God wanted it to do.

Family

Family

Describe your family.
Describe yourself.
Write or draw all of your family members in the circle.

God picked you especially for your family. He gave you special parents! He wants your family to be like a circle, full and never-ending, just like His love for you!

John 15:12 My command is this: Love each other as I have loved you.

Kindness

What is something nice someone has done for you?
Have you ever seen a friend be nice to another friend?
What makes people smile?
What is the silliest smile you can make on your face?
How can you make someone smile tomorrow?

Lord, smiles are so wonderful! Let me give lots of smiles tomorrow.
Thank you for smiling on me!

Luke 6:38 Give, and it will be given to you.

Do Your Best!

Once upon a time there was a boy who LOVED baseball. He loved to watch major league ballplayers and of course, he had a favorite team...The St. Louis Cardinals.
He loved the sound of his bat cracking against the ball then soaring over the fence.
One day he got the opportunity to pitch. Standing on the mound he threw pitch after pitch.
Some were balls, some were strikes and some even hit the batter (accidentally!) Pitch after pitch he got more frustrated. He hung his head low, down to his shoulders. His face looked worried and sad. He began sighing heavily. He slumped over. His eyebrows curved down making him look angry.
Can you act out how he was acting on the mound?
His parents spent the next 2 days sharing with him: "It doesn't matter if you throw strikes, balls or even if you hit a batter (accidentally!) What matters is how you act on the mound. Stay positive! It matters most that you do your very best!"
From that day on, he smiled, stood tall and threw the very best he could from the mound.

Lord, help me to always try my best. You made me the way I am, so help me be the best I can be. Thank you!

I LOVE ME!

Look in the mirror, what do you see?
What do you like most?
Is there anything you would like to change?
Draw a picture of yourself using as many colors as you can. Give it a title.

God made you very special. There is no one on earth just like you. You are one of a kind!

Genesis 1:27 God created man in his own image, in the image of God he created him; male and female he created them.

12

"U get what U get and U don't throw a fit!"

Have U ever heard this before?   Yes or no (circle one)
Have U ever thrown a fit?   Why?

Once upon a time there was a small boy. He was a very special person! He was only 3, but he thought he was so much older. He knew exactly what he wanted in life. He knew when he *wanted* a cup of juice and when he did not *want* a cup of juice. He knew when he *wanted* to swing, when he *wanted* to play baseball, and when he *wanted* to take a nap. He knew when he *wanted* to get up in the morning and what he *wanted* to eat. He especially knew when he *wanted* to give a hug.

Because he knew exactly what he wanted, it was so hard for him when he couldn't get what he wanted. If it was time to leave the house, but he was ready to ride his scooter, he would shout, "But I don't WANT to leave the house! I WANT to ride my scooter!"

One day the little boy wanted a lollipop. He got a blue one. But he wanted a red one. He threw a fit. He was crying and screaming. His older sister didn't get a treat and she told him, "You get what you get and you don't throw a fit!"

The little boy thought about it and understood that he needed to be thankful for what he was given because he was blessed to have the lollipop in the first place.

13

Coach

What is a coach?
Who is a coach to you?
Who is your teacher?
How do they help you?
When are you a coach?
Color a picture or write a short letter to a coach.

Lord, thank you for all of the people in my life! Help me to listen and learn from them.

Colossians 3:17   And whatever you do, whether in word or deed, do it all in the name of the Lord Jesus, giving thanks to God the Father through him.

3 Favorite Things to do with Dad

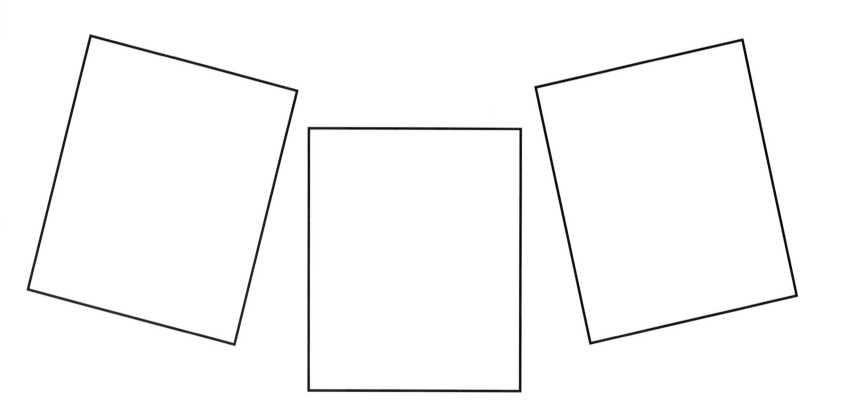

Dad

What do you like to do most with your dad?
How is he special?
Tell a funny story about your dad.

Draw or write your 3 favorite things you like to do most with your dad in the boxes.

Exodus 20:12 Honor your father and mother.

Happy Day!

What was the best thing that happened to you today?
What was the worst?
If you could have changed anything about today, what would it be?

Dear God, thank you for this day! Thank you for everyday. Stay with me all through the days. I will try to make everyday a good day. Amen

Psalm 118:24   This is the day the Lord has made; let us rejoice and be glad in it.

Growing Up!

Once upon a time there was a boy who wanted to be all grown up – FAST! Have you ever wished to be bigger? Is there someone older than you that you wanted to do things with or weren't able to do things with because they were older than you?

I am the younger one. I feel that way some times. I just wish I could be bigger! I have an older brother and he is the greatest! I would do anything for him. Sometimes I even stick up for him. When he is sick or gets into trouble, it makes me feel sad. He is taller than me. Now I've almost caught up to his height.

There are times when we have a hard time agreeing on things and we get mad at each other (but not for long). It is usually about sports. I guess it is because sometimes we see things differently and we both think we are better than the other one.

I think that is called being competitive.

When I want to play a board game I get it out, set it up, and then go on a search to find someone to play with me. I play my heart out!

When I'm "it" in freeze tag, I run and run until everyone is frozen. When I play catcher in baseball I throw down the mask and go after the ball every time!

I don't know why, but at times I put my "all" into what ever I do and really try my best.

I think it's called being passionate.

(Sometimes my passion gets a little excited and my parents give me a little pep talk to calm it down.)

Being the younger one, I want to keep up, but maybe not grow up too fast!

Love

Who do you love?
How has someone shown that they love you?
How do you show people that you love them?
God loves you, who else loves you?

Thank you God for loving me! Help me to love other people. Thank you for my family.

1 Chronicles 16:34 Give thanks to the Lord, for he is good; his love endures forever.

I Want That!

Have you ever wanted something so badly that it is all you could think about?
Did you get it?
How did you feel after you got it?
Is there something you really want right now?
Write it down here_____.
Why do you think you want it?

Dear Lord, help me to remember all that you have done for us. Thank you for what you have given me. You bless me always.

Galatians 2:20 Christ lives in me.

Good at Everything?

What is something you have learned that you have become really good at?
How did you get good at it?
Is there something else you would like to get better at?
Is everyone good at everything?

Lord, help me to know that you want me to do my best. You made me who I am and I don't always have to be good at everything.

Philippians 4:13 I can do everything through Him who gives me strength.

Different Homes have Different Rules

What rule do you like best in our house?
What rule do you NOT like best?
Why do we have rules?
What would be a funny rule we could make up and live by?

It is hard sometimes for me to understand that I am different from other people, Lord. Help me to know that you are looking out for me and protecting me. Remind me to listen to my parents and be respectful to them. They are protecting me too!

1 Timothy 3:4   He must manage his own family well and see that his children obey him with proper respect.

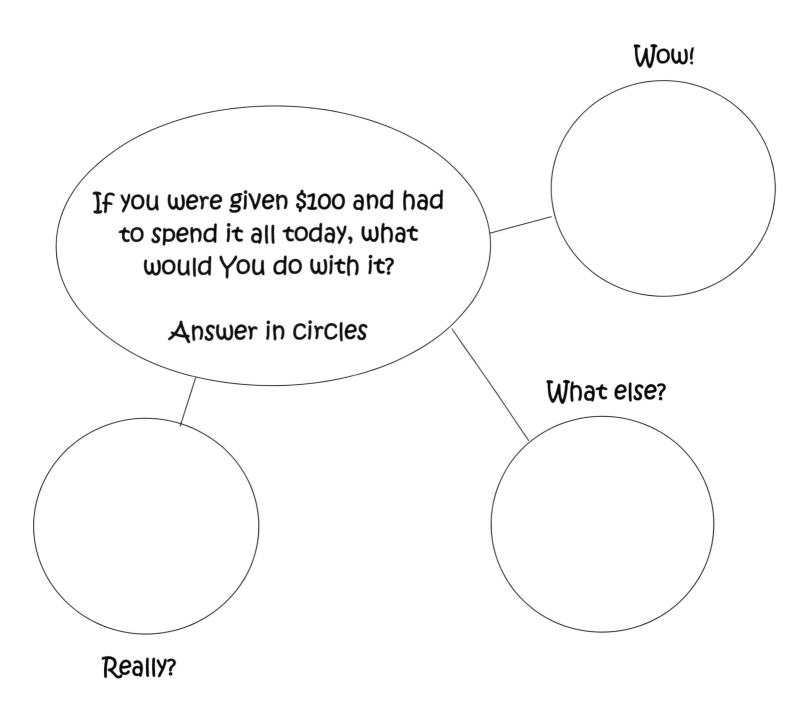

Wow!

If you were given $100 and had to spend it all today, what would You do with it?

Answer in circles

What else?

Really?

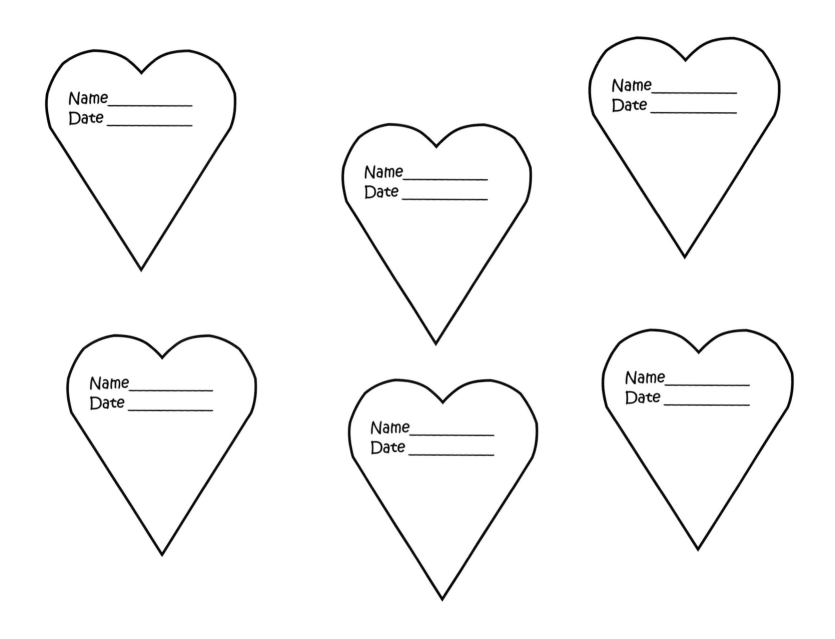

Name_____
Date _____

Name_____
Date _____

Name_____
Date _____

Name_____
Date _____

Name_____
Date _____

Name_____
Date _____

Circle Around

Sit in a circle on the floor with your family.
Tell each person what you like most about them.
Everyone take a turn.

Dear God, you have made each of us really special. There are many things that are different about each one of us, but there are also many things that are so wonderful about us! It is good to share with others what is wonderful about them. Thank you for my family!

Romans 12:6 We have different gifts, according to the grace given us.

Scary Times

What are you afraid of?
Share two times when you were scared.
What would have made you feel better?

Lord, everyone is afraid sometimes. Maybe a rainstorm, a new school, or bigger kids will make me scared. I know you are there to help me and protect me. Please stay with me and make me strong.

Hebrews 13:6   The Lord is my helper; I will not be afraid.

God's Embrace

Once upon a time a little boy was born. He had loving parents and grandparents. His grandparents made sure they were at all of his special events...baptism, birthdays, Christmas, and Thanksgiving. They were there sometimes when there wasn't a special event.

He was thankful to have such wonderful grandparents in his life. He knew each grandparent held a special place in his heart. He learned something from each one of them.

Do you have someone that means a lot to you? Do they teach you things?

This little boy learned a lot of things from his grandparents. He learned about golf, sportsmanship, fishing, vegetables (they grow in a garden, not a store), generosity, love of ice cream, beach vacations, dogs, reading, football, baseball, confidence, story telling, kindness, and most of all, no matter what, they would always love him!

When the little boy became a little older two of his grandparents went to heaven.

Of course, he did not understand why that happened and he really missed them. But he knew they were going to be all right because God is taking care of them. He said he has a piece of them in his heart that will always be with him.

They gave him that.

Every day there is something he will remember that he shared with one of his grandparents. And one day (maybe even today), he will be sharing what he has learned with someone else he loves.

What is something you have learned that you can share with someone you love?

Take 1 minute and think about this question...

What is something that is most special to you?

Why is it special?
Share 5 other things that are special to you.
Ask your parents what is special to them.

Dear Lord, thank you for all of my special gifts. Let me give thanks to you for all good things! Help me to always remember what is most important. Thank you!

James 1:17 Every good and perfect gift is from above, coming down from the Father of the heavenly lights, who does not change like shifting shadows."

You are Like Who you Hang Around

Who are your friends?
Can you name at least 3 good friends?
Who do you like to spend time with most?
What do you do if a friend does something and makes a bad choice?
How can you be a good friend to others?

Thank you God for my friends. Show me how to be a good friend to others. Help me to be kind and giving to everyone. Help me to talk to kids who may not have any one else to talk to. Let me smile and listen to them.

1 Corinthians 15:23 Do not be misled: Bad company corrupts good character.

MOM

What do you like most about your mom?
How is she special?
What do you like to do most with your mom?
Tell a funny story about your mom.

God, thank you for my mother! I know you picked me to be with her. She is a very special person. Help me to be thankful for all she does for me.

Exodus 20:12   Honor your father and mother.

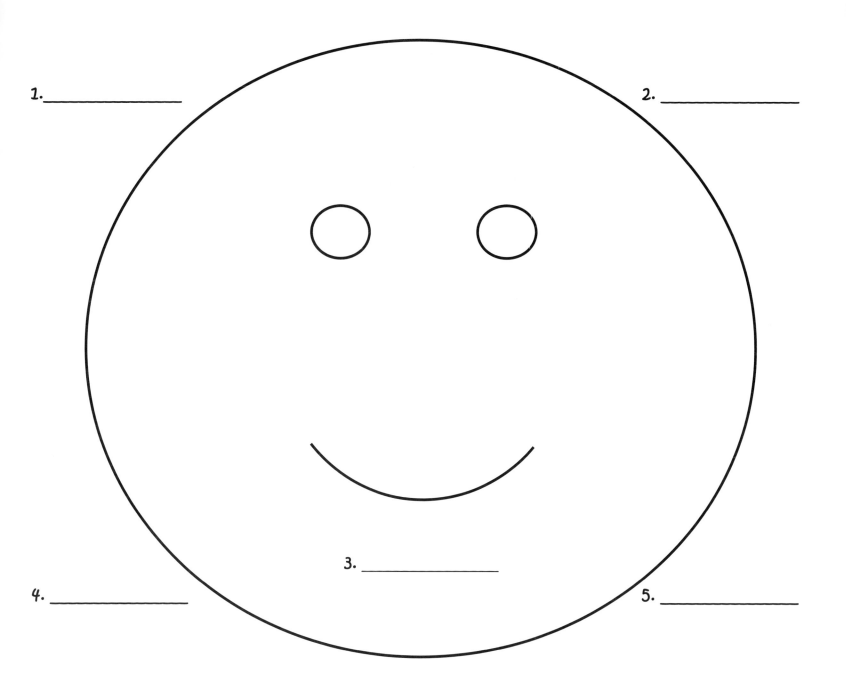

1._____

2._____

3. _____

4. _____

5. _____

Ways to Be Nice

How were you nice to someone today?
How did it make you feel?
What is something nice you could do tomorrow?
Tell about a time someone was very nice to you.
Fill in the 5 blanks with ways to be nice.

Lord, being nice and kind to other people is one way I can show your love for us. Let me remember how it feels when someone is nice to me, so I can be nice to others.

Matthew 7:12 So in everything, do to others what you would have them do to you.

Good Choice!

Has a friend or someone you know ever done something wrong?
What was it?
What would have been a better way to do it?
Is it sometimes hard to make the right choice?
When was a time you made a great choice?
Ask a parent to share a time with you when he/she made a great choice!

Dear Lord, help me remember that I can only control myself. I can't control my friends. Help me to make the right choices.

Colossians 2:13   He forgave us all our sins.

Listen

What does it mean to LISTEN?
How do you listen to your parents?
How do you listen to your teacher?
How do you listen to your brother or sister?
Can you listen with your eyes?
Who was the last person you listened to?
Who do you like to listen to the most?

Lord, I have heard that you gave us 2 ears and 1 mouth for a reason. That way we will take more time to care and listen to other people than to talk only about ourselves. Help me to learn to listen nicely to my parents, my teachers, my friends and especially to you!

Psalm 66:19 But God has surely listened and heard my voice in prayer.

Hero

Who is a hero?
What is a hero like?
How are you like a hero?

Lord, Jesus is our hero. He died for us so we could be with you forever. Thank you for sending Jesus to us!

John 3:16 For God so loved the world that he gave his one and only Son, that whoever believes in him shall not perish but have eternal life.

Forgiveness

Has anyone ever been mean to you?
What did they do?
What did you do when that happened?
Share a way you have been mean to someone else.
What does it mean to FORGIVE?

No one is perfect here on earth. We all do things wrong once in a while. Jesus asks us to forgive someone when he or she has been mean to us. That can be hard to do! The good news is that if WE are ever mean to someone, we can ask their forgiveness too!

Ephesians 4:32 Be kind and compassionate to one another, forgiving each other, just as in Christ God forgave you.

I Don't Feel Good!

Once upon a time there was a beautiful young girl. Her hair was dark brown with sparkling solid brown eyes. Her smile lit up the room. It was like a ray of sunshine that God created. She loved to do everything! She loved ballet, tap dance, acrobatics, coloring, softball, riding her bike, swimming, piano, singing and even school!
Do you like to do any of those things?
This wonderful girl didn't feel very good some times. Sometimes she was sick. Have you ever been sick? What did it feel like?
Her body didn't feel good a lot of the time. BUT, she kept doing all of the things she loved to do. She kept smiling and playing. She did her very best in everything!
She also asked God to help her. The next time you don't feel well, ask Him to help you and make you feel better!

Psalm 30:2   O Lord my God, I called to you for help and you healed me.

<u>List of Thankfulness</u>

<u>1.</u>

<u>2.</u>

<u>3.</u>

<u>4.</u>

<u>5.</u>

<u>6.</u>

<u>7.</u>

<u>8.</u>

<u>9.</u>

<u>10.</u>

Thank You!

What does it mean when we say "Thank You?"
List 10 things you are thankful for.

Lord, Thank you so much for our home and our family. Keep watch over us and protect us all. Please be with those who are not near us.

1 Thessalonians 5:16-18 Be joyful always; pray continually; give thanks in all circumstances, for this is God's will for you in Christ Jesus.

LOVE   GOODNESS

SELF-CONTROL

                        JOY   PATIENCE

                              GENTLENESS

        FAITHFULLNESS

                        KINDNESS   PEACE

Fruit of The Spirit

Galatians 5:22-23 But the fruit of the spirit is love, joy, peace, patience, kindness, goodness, faithfulness, gentleness, and self-control. Against such things there is no law.

What does each of these words mean? If you don't know, ask your parents to help you understand. God wants us to try to be all of these things. It may seem hard but you can do it!

Lord, these words are wonderful! I want to live in happiness. Help me to remember to love other people. Help me to remember that you love me. Help me to try every day to live by the fruit of the spirit.

Draw and **color** a fruit around each of the words on the opposite page. Make it colorful!

I Want to Be a Fireman!

Do you want to be a fireman when you grow up?
What do you want to do when you grow up?
Where do you want to live when you grow up?
What will be your favorite thing to do when you grow up?

Lord, thank you for my life and my family. You have blessed us all because we have each other. Help me to listen to you as I grow up so I can follow your plan for me!

Jeremiah 29:11 "For I know the plans I have for you," declares the Lord, "plans to prosper you and not harm you, plans to give you hope and a future."